The Little Book of

WRINKLIES
JOKES

D1639227

First published in Great Britain in 2009 by Prion

an imprint of the Carlton Publishing Group
20 Mortimer Street
London W1T 3JW

10 9 8 7 6 5 4 3 2 1

Text copyright © 2009 Mike Haskins and Clive Whichelow
Design copyright © 2009 Carlton Publishing Group

A catalogue record for this book is available from the British Library

ISBN 978-1-85375-723-5

Printed in China

The material in this book was previously published in *Wrinklies Joke Book*

The Little Book of
WRINKLIES
JOKES

By Mike Haskins and Clive Whichelow

PRION

INTRODUCTION

Never stop laughing – it'll add years to your life!

An old man tells a friend, "I've got good news and bad news. The good news is I've finally discovered the Fountain of Youth." "What's the bad news?" asks his friend. "At my age," says the first old man, "I've forgotten what I wanted it for."

Two old men are talking. "You know, you're only as old as you feel," says the first. "Oh," says the second. "In that case how come I'm still alive when I'm 150 years old?"

The ages of man – in fruit. At 20, a man is like a coconut: he has so much to offer, but so little to give. At 30, he's like a durian: dangerous, but strangely delicious. At 40, he's like a watermelon: big, round and juicy. At 50, he's like a Satsuma: he only comes once every year. At 60, he's more like a raisin: dried out, wrinkled and cheap.

The ages of woman – in balls. At 18, she's a football: 22 men are running after her from all directions. At 28, she's a hockey ball: 8 men are panting to get her. At 38, she's a golf ball: there's only one man's after her now. By 48, she's a table-tennis ball: two guys are doing their damnedest to get rid of her.

A census taker knocks on an old woman's front door. She answers his questions until he asks how old she is. "I'm sorry," says the old woman, "but I don't believe it's lady-like to tell anyone my age." "Oh dear," says the census taker, "that does make things rather difficult." "Well, I'm the same age as Mr and Mrs Hill who live next door." "That's fine," says the census taker, "I'll just put down, 'as old as the hills.'"

When you're three years old, success is not peeing in your pants. When you're 17, success is having a driving licence. When're 20, success is having sex. When you're 30, success is having cash. When you're 40, success is having a big, impressive house. When you're 50, success is having cash. When you're 60, success is having sex. When you're 70, success is having a driving licence. When you're 80, success is not peeing in your pants.

An old boy goes along to his school reunion and all his old spend the evening talking about their failing health and comparing grisly notes. "One was on about his heart problems," he told his wife when he got home. "Another was discussing his kidney transplant, and another was banging on about his liver problems..." "Oh dear," said his wife, "it doesn't sound so much like a school reunion as an organ recital."

An old man goes for a thorough examination at the doctor's. After it's over, the old man asks, "Well, doctor, how do I stand?" "To be honest," says the doctor, "that's what's puzzling me."

An old lady is having a check-up from her doctor for her asthma. He asks a few questions and notes down her croaky replies. Finally he asks, "And what about the wheeze?" "Oh they're fine," says the old lady, "I went three times last night."

An old man goes to a private practice. "I'll examine you for £100," says the doctor. "Go ahead then," says the old man, "and if you find £100, you can keep it."

Elsie goes to the doctors suffering a whole range of aches, pains, and ailments. The doctor examines her and says, "Well, Mrs Cartwright, I know you must be in some discomfort, but there's not a lot I can do. You're 75 years old, and well, I can't make you any younger you know." "I'm not bothered about getting any younger," says Elsie, "I just want to make sure I get a bit older."

Old Harry goes to see his doctor for a rectal examination. "Ooh," says Harry, "that was a bit uncomfortable." "Sorry," says the doctor. "I had to use two fingers, not one." "What was that for?" asks Harry. "I thought I better get a second opinion," says the doctor.

An old man been feeling ill for a little while so he goes to his doctor. After a while, the doctor calls him in to hear the results of the tests. "I'm afraid I have bad news. You're dying and you don't have much time," says the doctor. "Oh no," says the old man. "How long have I got?" "Ten." says the doctor. "Ten? Ten what? Months? Weeks? What exactly?" "... nine... eight... seven... six..."

Old Fred goes to the doctor's. The doctor examines him, consults some books and papers, then says, "I'm afraid I've got some bad news for you, Fred," and hands him a small bottle of pills. "You're going to have to take these pills for the rest of your life." "That's not so bad," says Fred. "Yes it is," says the doctor. "I'm afraid that you're not going to be needing any repeat prescriptions."

A traffic policeman pulls over a lady for speeding. "Madam," he says as he goes up to her car window. "When I saw you tearing down the street. I guessed 65 as a minimum." "That's ridiculous, officer," says the woman. "I'm 54. It's these damn glasses – they put ten years on me."

Two women are talking. "I think 30 is a great age to be," says the first. "Yes," says her friend, "particularly when in reality you're 45."

Two old ladies are having a natter about their favourite subject, their various medical conditions. The first tells the second, "The doctor says I need another operation but I can't afford to get it done privately and there's a 12-month waiting list on the NHS." "That's a disgrace," says her friend. "What is the world coming to, I ask you. Still never mind. We'll just have to talk about your old operation for another year."

A 90-year-old man goes to his doctor and says, "Oh doctor, it's my right knee. It's awfully stiff and painful." The doctor has a look and says, "I'm afraid there's not much I can do. You've had that knee for 90 years now, so you can't expect too much." "Nonsense," says the old man. "I've had my left knee for exactly the same length of time and there's nothing wrong with that one at all."

A posh old woman is talking to her friend. She tells her, "My husband is now so elderly and infirm, I have to watch him all day and night." "But I thought you'd hired a young nurse to take care of him," says her friend. "Yes, I have," says the old woman, "and a very sweet and attentive young thing she is too. That's precisely why I've got to keep an eye on him."

An old lady was having some persistent stomach problems, so the doctor told her to drink tepid water with a teaspoon of Epsom salts an hour before breakfast every morning. After a month she was no better so went back to the doctor. "Did you drink the water an hour before breakfast every morning?" he asked. "No, doctor," she replied. "I'm sorry. I did my best, but I couldn't manage more than 20 minutes."

In the waiting room at the surgery a vast crowd of people were waiting for their appointments while the doctor seemed to be working at a snail's pace. After two hours' wait, one old man slowly got up and shuffled towards the door. Everyone turned to look at him, so he shook his head and said, "Given the rate he's working, I may as well just go home and die a natural death."

A life insurance salesman knocks at the door of a 90-year-old man. He gives him the hard sell, but the old man is a bit wary about the cost, which at his age isn't cheap. After about 45 minutes of haggling on the doorstep, the salesman finally says, "Look, I'll tell you what, have a think about it, sleep on it tonight, and if you wake up in the morning give me a ring, OK?"

Old Bill goes to his doctor's and says, "Doctor, my memory is terrible. I can't remember anything." "OK," says the doctor. "Tell me all about it." "All about what?" says Bill.

Two old ladies meet for a weekly game of cards. Halfway through their game one week, one says, "I'm so sorry. We've been friends for sixty years, but I just can't think what your name is. Would you remind me please?" The other old lady sits staring at her for a few moments. "I've offended you haven't I?" says the first old lady. "No," says the second, "I can't remember what it is myself at the moment."

A woman notices an old man sitting on a park bench sobbing his eyes out. She goes over and asks what's wrong. "I have a 22-year-old wife," says the old man. "Every single morning she insists on making mad passionate love with me before she gets up and makes breakfast for me." "OK," says the woman. The old man goes on, "She makes my lunch for me, does my washing, my ironing, keeps the house beautiful and still has the energy to make love as soon as I get home in the afternoon." "I see," says the woman. "Every evening she cooks me a delicious gourmet meal which she serves with wine and my favourite dessert before doing all the dishes and making love to me again until bedtime." "Fine," says the woman, thinking to herself that the old boy must be very rich. "So why are you sitting here sobbing?" "I've forgotten where I live," says the old man.

Two old gentlemen were talking whilst their wives tinkered in the kitchen. One said, "Last night we to a great new restaurant. I really recommend it." His friend said, "What's it called?" The first man thought, then finally said, "What's the name of the flower you give to a love? You know, red, with thorns." "A rose?" "Of course!" replied the man. He turned towards the kitchen and yelled, "Rose, where did we eat last night?"

An old lady and her husband are always arguing over which of them has the better memory. "OK," says the old lady, "if you want to prove your memory's not so bad, go and get me a cup of tea." Off goes her husband to the kitchen, only to return ten minutes later with a steaming bowl of porridge. "You idiot!" says the old woman. "Where the hell are my eggs!"

An old actor falls on hard times because he forgets his lines. Eventually he finds a theatre where they are prepared to give him a chance. The director says, "This is the most important role, and it has only one line. You walk on to the stage at the opening carrying a rose. You hold the rose to your nose with just one finger and thumb, sniff the rose deeply and then say, 'Ah, the sweet aroma of my mistress.'" The actor is thrilled. Finally, the time comes. The curtain goes up, the actor walks onto the stage, lifts his hands to his face and sniffs mightily, and with great passion delivers the line, "Ah, the sweet aroma of my mistress." The theatre erupts. The audience is screaming with laughter, but the director is steaming! "You fool!" he cries. "You've ruined me!" The old actor is bewildered, "What happened, did I forget my line?" "No!" screams the director. "You forgot the rose!"

An old man visits his doctor and says, "Oh, doctor. I've got a terrible problem. I seem to have developed an awful memory. I can't remember where I left my car. I can't remember how I got here. I can't even remember where I live or whether I'm married or not. Can you help me, doctor?" "I can," says the doctor, "but I'm afraid that you're going to have to pay me in advance."

In a retirement home two old men are eating breakfast one morning. One notices something in the other one's ear. "I say, old man," says the first, "did you know you've got a suppository in your ear?" His friend pulls it out and looks at it. "Thank goodness you noticed that," he says. "I wondered where that had got to. Now if only I could think where I've put my hearing aid...."

A 65-year-old woman has IVF and has a baby. As soon as she gets home, her sister calls round and asks, "Can I see the new arrival?" "Not yet," says the mother. Half an hour later, the sister asks, "Come on! Please can I see him?" "No," says the mother. "You've got to wait until he cries." "I don't understand. Why?" "Because," says the 65-year-old, "at the moment I can't remember where I've left him."

Three absent-minded professors were at a bus stop. They got so engrossed in their conversation, they didn't notice the bus arrive. As it got ready to leave, they finally noticed, and dashed for it. Two managed to hop on, but the third sadly failed. A stranger tried to cheer him up. "Two out of three of you got on. That's pretty good." "It would be," said the professor, "but they only came to see me off."

Old Sid tells a friend, "My wife has a terrible memory. She never forgets a single thing."

Joyce tells her friend Glenda, "I'm going to divorce Harry." "Why's that?" asks Glenda. "Because," says Joyce, "he has a rotten memory." "OK," says Glenda, "but why divorce him just because he has a bad memory?" "Because," says Joyce, "Every time he sees an attractive young woman he forgets he's married to me!"

An old lady is waiting to see the doctor. When she gets unsteadily to her feet, using a walking stick, one of the other patients notices she is bent almost double. Ten minutes later the door opens and the old woman walks out completely upright. "My goodness!" says the other patient. "That's amazing! What did the doctor give you, some sort of miracle cure?" "No," says the old lady, "he gave me a longer stick."

Three old men who are all hard of hearing are playing golf one morning. One says to another, "Windy, isn't it?" "No," says the second man, "it's Thursday." The third man then pipes up, "Yes. So am I! Let's get a beer!"

An old guy who's been deaf for years finally gets a great new hearing aid from the doctor. The check-up is a month later. The doctor says, "Yes, your hearing is good again. Your family must be really pleased at the improvement." "Oh I haven't told them about it yet," says the elderly gentleman. "I just sit around and listen to what they're all saying to each other. So far I've changed my will five times!"

An old man worries his wife is going deaf. He walks up close to her and says "Can you hear me?" His wife doesn't answer. So the old man gets a bit closer again and says even more loudly, "Can you hear me?" Again there is no answer, so he tries once more, standing even closer and shouting, "CAN YOU HEAR ME!!!" And his wife replies, "FOR THE THIRD TIME, YES I CAN BLOODY HEAR YOU!!!!"

While it may not be entirely true to say that all the people who live in Bournemouth are getting on a bit, it is one of the few places where the shops on the high street have to have their windows made from bifocal lenses.

An ageing snake goes to see his doctor. "Doctor, I need something for my eyes," says the snake, "I don't see so well these days." The doctor gives him a pair of glasses. Two weeks later, the snake is back, asking for anti-depressants. The doctor says, "What's the problem? Didn't the glasses help you?" "They're fine," says the snake. "But I just found out I've been living with a garden hose for the past couple of years!"

Old Jack gets in from a round of golf. "How was your game, dear?" asks his wife, Beryl. "Well, I was hitting pretty well, but my eyesight's so bad now I couldn't see where the ball went," answers Jack. "It's making the damn game impossible to play." "What can you expect," says Beryl. "You're 75 years old!" "Oh, I know that," says Jack sadly. "Why don't you take my brother Arthur along?" asks Beryl. "But he's 85 and he doesn't even play golf," says Jack. "Never mind," says Beryl, "he's got perfect eyesight so he'll be able to watch the ball for you."

The next day Jack tees off with Arthur looking on. Jack takes a swing and the ball disappears down the middle of the fairway. "Did you see where it went?" asks Jack. "I certainly did," says Arthur. "Excellent," says Jack. "So where is it?" "Er...." says Arthur peering off into the distance. "No. Sorry. I've forgotten."

A flat-chested young woman can't find
a bra small enough, and eventually tries
a little backstreet lingerie shop. The old
dear behind the counter is short-sighted
and a bit deaf, so the woman has trouble
explaining what she wants. Eventually
she simply unbuttons her blouse and
shouts "Have you got anything for
these?" The old woman squints at her and
says, "Oh dear. Try Clearasil, love. My
granddaughter swears by it."

An old couple are watching a documentary programme about healthcare on the television. "I never want to end up like that," says the old man pointing at the television. "I don't want to end up living in a vegetative state, dependent on some machine and fluids from a bottle. If that ever happens to me, pull the plug." His wife glares at him, then gets up, unplugs the TV, and pours the bottle of beer down the sink.

Two old men are shuffling down the street. The man on the left is dragging his right foot, the other is dragging his left foot. The man on the right says to the man on the left, "What happened to you?" "War wound," he replies. "Normandy beach 1944. So," he says, indicating the other old man's foot, "what about you?" "I trod in some dog muck a couple of streets back," says the other.

Three old men are playing cards and decide they should get some beer in. They draw straws and Norman is given the money to go and buy some beer from the pub. Half an hour passes with no sign of Norman. One of the other old men says, "I'm beginning to think Norm's run off with our money." Norman immediately pipes up from just outside the front door, "Hey! Any more of that and I won't go!"

A bus driver notices in his mirror that his passengers are in uproar. He stops the bus and goes to investigate. He discovers an elderly man crawling up and down the bus looking for something on the floor. "What on earth do you think you're doing?" asks the bus driver. "You're being a nuisance to all the other people on the bus." "I can't help that," says the old man, "I'm looking for my chewing gum." "What do you mean you're looking for your chewing gum?" says the driver. "You're making this amount of fuss over some old chewing gum that's been on the floor of the bus which you wouldn't be able to use again anyway." "That doesn't matter," says the old man, "but I've still got to find my chewing gum. It's vitally important that I find my chewing gum!" "Well, what the hell's so special about this chewing gum?" asks the driver. "My teeth are still in it," says the old man.

An old lady goes to her dentist to have her dentures adjusted for the umpteenth time. Like every time, she insists, "These dentures still don't fit." "What are you talking about?" says the dentist. "We've adjusted them over and over again. How can they possibly still not fit?" "You don't believe they don't fit! I'll prove it to you!" says the old woman. "I've brought the tumbler from the side of my bed with me..."

An old man sees a little boy sitting at the side of the road crying his eyes out. "What's the matter there, son?" asks the old codger. "You should be off playing games and having fun. Why are you crying?" "I'm crying," says the little boy, "because I can't do what the big boys do." The old man looks at him for a moment, then sits down next to him on the kerb and starts crying too.

As a man gets older, he comes to the understanding there are basically only three styles for his hair – parted, unparted, and departed.

Two elderly ladies were discussing the upcoming dance to be held that weekend at the country club. "It says that we're supposed to wear something that matches our husband's hair, so I'm wearing black," said Mrs. Smith. "Oh my word," said Mrs. Jones, "I'd better not go."

The best way to get an ageing man to do anything is to suggest he's far too old to be capable of it.

Two old men are walking down the street together when they see a pair of hot teenage girls walk by. "Oh," says the first, "I wish I was 20 years older." "You stupid old fool," says his friend. "You're 75 years old. You don't wish you were 20 years older. You wish you were 20 years younger." "No," says the first. "I really don't. I mean 20 years older. That way, I'd be past caring."

An old man goes to the doctor's for an examination. The doctor checks him over, takes his pulse and blood pressure, and cheerfully pronounces him fit as a fiddle. On his way out of the surgery, the old man has a massive heart attack and drops dead on the spot. The doctor leaps into action and tells the receptionist, "Quick! Turn him round and make it look like he was just walking in!"

A man is recovering after major heart surgery. The surgeon gives him strict instructions, tells him he mustn't drink, smoke or eat badly, and advises him to get at least eight hours of sleep a night. Finally, the patient asks, "What about my sex life? Will it be all right for me to have intercourse?" "Yes," says the surgeon. "As long as it's just with your wife. Nothing too exciting, you understand."

A very old man was given some medicine. "This is strong stuff," said the doctor, "Take some the first day, then skip a day, and so on." Some time later, he saw the old man's wife in the street and asked after him. The doctor was horrified to hear that the man had died. "I didn't think the medicine was that strong," said the doctor ruefully. "It wasn't the medicine," said the widow. "It was all that skipping."

An old man is waiting for a heart transplant when the doctor comes to see him. "Good news!" he says. "We've found a donor. In fact, you have a choice. There's a young sportsman who was very fit, or a 70-year-old lawyer." "I'll have the lawyer's heart please," says the old man. "Did you hear me?" asks the doctor. "It's from a 70-year-old lawyer." "Yes," says the patient. "So it's never been used."

Archie and Agnes were married for 60 years, so when Archie died, Agnes couldn't face life without him. She found Archie's old army revolver in the drawer and phoned her local hospital to find out exactly where her heart was. She was told it was just below the left breast. She poured herself a large gin and fired the fateful shot. Half an hour later she was admitted to casualty with a gunshot wound to her left knee.

An old couple are in the middle of the congregation at church one Sunday. Halfway through the service, the old man leans over and quietly murmurs to his his wife, "I think I just broke wind, and right in the middle of the vicar's talk, too. Luckily it was a silent one. But do you think I should do anything?" "Yes," says his wife. "You need to change the batteries in your hearing aid!"

An old lady goes to her doctor and asks what can be done about her terrible constipation. "Doctor," she says, "I haven't moved my bowels for more than a week." "I see," says the doctor. "Have you done anything about it?" "Oh, yes," says the old lady, "I sit there for half an hour every morning." "No no," says the doctor. "I mean, do you take anything?" "Yes, of course," says the old lady. "I take a magazine!"

Three old men are comparing ailments. "Every morning," says one, "at seven o'clock, I get up to urinate but I never can." The second says, "Ha! Every morning at eight o'clock I get up to defecate. It never works." The third says, "Every morning at seven o'clock I urinate and defecate at eight o'clock." "You've got no problem then," says the first man. "Yes I have," says the third man. "I don't wake up till nine."

Have you heard about the new bra they've invented for women in later life? They call it the sheep dog. That's because it rounds them up and gets them pointing in the same direction.

Two ageing ladies are long time rivals.
They meet at at their country club. "Why,
my dear," says the first, "don't tell me
those are real pearls." "Of course," says
the second. "You may say that," says the
first woman, "but the only way I could tell
for certain would be to bite them." "Well
I'd be happy for you to do that," says the
second woman. "The only trouble is you'd
need real teeth."

Keith asks his girlfriend Karen to marry him and she says yes, but on one condition – that he buys her a solid gold boy scout pocket knife. He asks around, he looks on the Internet, he tries everywhere, but he can't find a solid gold boy scout knife anywhere. They're just not made. That doesn't really surprise him all that much, but he really wants to marry Karen, so he goes to a jeweller and asks the woman to make him one. It is very expensive, but when it's ready he presents it to Karen, who agrees to marry him. "Why did you want a solid gold boy scout knife?" asked Keith. Karen says, "I'm going to put it away somewhere safe, then, when I'm old and grey and wrinkled with half my teeth missing, and my boobs sagging and no man will look at me twice, I'll get it out. Because let's be honest here, a good boy scout will do absolutely anything legal for a solid gold pocket knife."

You don't know even the first thing about real embarrassment until your hip sets off a metal detector.

An old man goes into hospital to have a hip replacement. The hospital remove his old hip, and fit him with a new plastic one that has a sensitive spring-based action. When he gets home, his grandchildren are delighted to discover every time they push granddad's head down, he takes a penalty.

In the town centre a slightly odd looking old man keeps wandering around yelling to no-one in particular. "Why does that man keep doing that?" asks a passer-by. "Oh, that's old Mr Jones," says a local. "He can't help it. He's just talking to himself in the street again." "Well, if he's talking to himself," says the passer-by, "why does he have to shout so much?" "He has to," says the local. "He's deaf."

An old man sees a psychiatrist. Afterwards, the psychiatrist speaks with the old man's wife. "Your husband may be psychotic," says the psychiatrist. "He thinks God switches the toilet light on for him at night when he opens the door, and turns it off again when he's done." "Ah," says the old lady. "You recognize the problem do you?" says the psychiatrist. "I certainly do," says the old lady. "He's been weeing in the fridge again."

Two paramedics picked up a 92-year-old man who had become seriously disoriented, to take him to hospital for evaluation. En route to hospital, they questioned the old man to determine his level of awareness. Leaning close, one asked, "Sir, do you know what we're doing right now?" The old man slowly looked up at him, then gazed out the ambulance window. "Oh," he replied, "I'd say about 50, maybe 55 or so."

Three elderly women are boasting about their grown up sons. "My son is lovely," says one. "He just gave me an expenses-paid trip to Europe." "That's nothing," says the second woman. "Yesterday, my son bought me a new Mercedes!" "Ha!" scoffs the third. "My son goes to a top Harley Street psychiatrist, he pays him £500 an hour, he sits there all afternoon and you know the only thing he talks about: me!"

A man asks his doctor if he will live to be 100. The doctor looks him over and asks, "Do you smoke or drink?" "No," replies the man. "I've never smoked and I never get drunk." "Do you gamble, drive fast cars and fool around with women?" inquired the doctor. "Of course not," says the man. "I've never done anything like that." "Well then," says the doctor. "What the hell do you want to live to 100 for?"

On Alf's 105th birthday, a reporter interviews him. "That's amazing," says the reporter. "What is your secret?" Alf answers, "Well, I never drank, I never smoked, I ran five miles every morning, and I always ate fresh fruit and vegetables." "Well that's fantastic, but I understand your twin brother Jim did the same, and died at 55. Is that true?" "Yep," says Alf. "But his problem was he didn't keep at it long enough."

A little boy is sitting on a bus eating a chocolate bar. As soon as he finishes it, he fishes around inside his pockets, digs out another one, and starts making his way through that. Then he has a third and a fourth, and a fifth. When he starts eating the sixth an old man sitting nearby says, "I don't think that's a very good idea, young man." "Why?" asks the boy. "It's bad for your teeth," said the old man. "It'll also make you fat and give you spots, and when you're older you might have heart problems. It can even give you diabetes, and that can make you go blind, or end up with you having to have your legs cut off." "Well," says the boy, unwrapping yet another bar of chocolate, "my granddad lived to be 102." "And did he eat half a dozen chocolate bars in a row ever day?" asks the old man. "No," snaps the boy. "Most of the time he just minded his own bloody business."

Tom swore by liver salts. He had a glass
after every meal, every day of his life.
Finally he died at the grand old age of 95.
At the funeral, the mourners had to beat
his liver to death with a stick.

Old Max joins a seniors' gym. The instructor says, "Max, it's amazing you're 70. From your shape, I would have put you at 55. How do you do it?" "Lack of stress," says Max. "Early in our marriage, the wife and I decided that if we started to argue, she'd go to the bedroom and I'd go into the garden." "Well," says the instructor, "how has that helped?" "I've been out in the fresh air for 50 years."

A man asks his elderly father what his secret was for living such a long life. "I'll tell you, son," says the old man. "Every morning I sprinkle a little bit of gun powder on my cereal." The man follows this advice to the letter. Amazingly it works. When he finally dies, aged 100, he leaves 14 children, 28 grandchildren, 35 great-grandchildren and a 15 foot hole in the wall of the crematorium.

A woman notices a little wizened old man rocking in a chair in his back garden. "You look so happy," she calls across to him. "What's your secret?" "I just enjoy life," he croaks back. "I smoke 60 cigarettes a day. I drink a case of whisky a week, I don't worry about what I eat and I never exercise." "That's amazing," says the woman. "So how old are you?" "Twenty-six," says the man.

"You know I exercise every single day," says an old man to his friend, a smug note in his voice. "So you know what that means." "Yes," says his friend. "I know exactly what it means. When we die you'll be much healthier than I am."

An old lady decides her body has got just too far out of shape, so she joins a fitness club to do some exercise. She head to the local fitness centre and signs on to do an aerobics class for senior citizens. On her first day she bends, twists, gyrates, jumps up and down and perspires for an hour. But, by the time she manages to get her leotard on, the class has finished.

Old Ned says his doctor told him to take up jogging and it would add ten years to his life. He's only been doing it two weeks and it's worked. He already feels ten years older.

An old lady of 95 goes to a gym and asks the instructor there if she can join the aerobics class. "Ooh, I don't know," says the instructor, who is understandably nervous at the prospect. "I'm not sure whether that's a very good idea." He looks her up and down and asks, "How flexible are you?" "Oh, don't worry, I'm very flexible," replies the old lady. "I just can't do Wednesday mornings, that's all."

You can take up jogging and it will help you live longer. Unfortunately it will feel absolutely awful. So that way it will help your life seem to last even longer still.

Old John wants to get his weight down, so he joins his local health club and tries the running machine. On his first day, he manages to lose one and a half stone. Unfortunately this is because the machine tears his leg off.

A woman accompanied her husband to the doctor's office. After his check-up, the doctor called the wife into his office alone. He said, "Your husband is suffering from a very severe disease, compounded by stress. You are his only chance. Each morning, make him a healthy breakfast. Try to be pleasant in general, and make sure he stays in a good mood. For lunch make him a nutritious meal. For dinner prepare something nice and healthy again. Don't burden him with chores, and don't discuss your problems with him, it will only make his stress worse. Most importantly, make love to him several times a week. If you can do this for the next eight weeks, I think your husband should regain his health completely." The woman took all of this on board, nodding thoughtfully. On the way home, the husband asked his wife, "What did the doctor say?" "I'm afraid you're going to die," she replied.

An old dying man is lying in bed, waiting with resignation for the inevitable end to come. One day he feels his senses begin to slightly revive as the smell of home baking comes wafting up the stairs and sets his mouth watering. With his last remaining strength he manages to pull himself out of bed and slowly and painfully struggles his way down the stairs and through the house, to the kitchen. There he finds his wife has been busily baking a delicious looking chocolate cake. "Oh my dear," says the dying old man, "That really is lovely of you. You've gone to the trouble of making me my very favourite cake." Just as he's about to cut himself a slice, his wife suddenly whacks his hand with a wooden spoon. "What's the matter with you?" asks the dying man." "Get your hands off that!" his wife tells him. "That's for the funeral!"

A bin man is on his rounds. As usual most of the bins have been left ready on the kerb but one old lady has forgotten to put hers out. Hearing the lorry pass by she runs out in her dressing gown and curlers and calls out, "Am I too late for the collection?" "Of course not, love," says the bin man, emptying another load into the back of the truck. "Come on! Hop in!"

A vicar is visiting an elderly parishioner and her pet parrot. The vicar says, "Forgive me, but why have you tied ribbons to his legs?" "Well," says the old lady. "If I pull the left ribbon he sings 'Abide With Me'. And if I pull on the right ribbon he sings 'Kumbayah'. "Wonderful!" chuckles the vicar. "What if you pull both at the same time?" "I fall off the damn perch you idiot," says the parrot.

An old lady orders a new carpet for her living room and a man turns up to fit it for her. It takes ages to fit the carpet into all the corners of the room, tack all the egdes down, and get all the various pieces of furniture back into their proper placcs. After he's finally finished with it, the man feels in his pocket for his packet of cigarettes and finds they're missing. He then notices a lump in the middle of the old lady's new carpet. "Oh no!" he says to himself. "I've dropped my fags and laid the carpet on top of them." In the end he decides the easiest thing is to get a hammer and gently tap the lump until it's completely flat. Just as he's got the bulge level, the old lady walks in with his pack of cigarettes in her hand. "Look!" she says. "You must have dropped these in the hall. Now I wonder if you could help me to find something. My pet budgie seems to have gone missing somewhere...."

A lady had a beautiful cat that she adored. One evening as she sat stroking it by the fireside, she dreamed of her cat turning into a handsome prince. Suddenly there was a flash of light, and lo and behold, there stood before her the most handsome prince anyone could possibly imagine.

The prince took her hand in his and murmured, "Aren't you sorry now that you took me to the vet last week?"

An old man tells his wife their dog is aging badly. "I think Rover is getting a bit old," he says, "he seems to be going deaf." "Absolute nonsense!" says his wife. "Just watch this! Rover, sit! ... Oh. Maybe you're right. Fetch the shovel and clean that up!"

An old lady is given a computer. Her son sets it up and demonstrates how to access the internet and search for information. "I'm not sure about this," says the old lady. "It's easy, Mum," says her son. "Just pretend the search engine is a person you're talking to. Ask it a question, press return and it'll answer anything you want." The old lady types into Google: "Hello. How are Auntie Ginnie's varicose veins?"

For the first time in years, an old man goes to the cinema. After buying his ticket, he stops at a kiosk to buy some popcorn. He is astonished at the price he is charged and tells the popcorn seller, "Last time I came to the cinema, a bag of popcorn only cost sixpence!" "Well, you're certainly going to enjoy the film this evening," says the young woman brightly. "They've got sound now and everything!"

Two ageing ladies are talking in the beauty parlour. "I've always had a nice firm chin," says one. "Yes," says the other, "and I see the firm has taken on a couple of partners."

Two old men are talking. The first says, "It's a funny old thing, the way that time can affect women. Back in the 1960s, my wife used to spend all her time and money trying to make herself look like Elizabeth Taylor." "What about now?" asks his friend. "Well, that's the thing," says the first old man. "Now she spends all her time and money trying NOT to look like Elizabeth Taylor."

She doesn't show her age, but if you look under her make-up it's there.

A little boy sees his grandmother in a face mask and asks, "What's that for?" "To make me more beautiful," says the grandmother, removing the mask. "Hmm," says the boy, concentrating really hard. "It hasn't worked."

A woman goes to a health centre for a week of beauty treatments. She gets home revitalized, and asks her husband, "So, if you didn't know me, how old would you say I was?" Her husband says, "From your skin, 26. From your hair, 20. And from your body..." The woman giggles girlishly and says, "You old flatterer, don't you think you're overdoing it?" "Hold on," says the husband, "I haven't added them up yet."

An old couple are getting ready to go out one night. The old man admires his wife when she's finished, clearly impressed with the results. "Wow," he says, "You look great." "Thank you," she says. "Yes," says the old man, "it must have taken you ages."

An old man tells his friend, "My wife is still as beautiful as the first time I saw her." "That's nice," says his friend. The old man says, "It takes her a couple of hours in the morning to get there, mind."

Two old men are chatting. "My wife tried putting on a mudpack to make herself attractive." "Did it work?" asks his friend. "It did for a bit," says the old man. "Then it fell off."

An ageing woman is worrying about the cosmetic surgery she has booked. "Is it going to hurt?" she asks her doctor. "Yes," he says, "I'm afraid it will – but not until you receive my invoice."

A definition of unhappiness: a woman who has her face lifted only to find an identical one lurking underneath.

Two men are sitting in a pub and opposite them is an attractive, young looking woman sitting on her own sipping a glass of wine. One of the men indicates the woman and says, "I reckon that woman has had plastic surgery, you know. Probably even a face-lift." The other one says, "How can you tell?" And the first man replies "Every time she crosses her legs her mouth suddenly snaps shut."

A man tells his friend, "My wife went in for a face lift operation last week." "Did it work?" asks the friend. "Not really," says the man. "When they saw what was under it, they dropped it again."

Two women are sitting in the old people's home bitching about the other inmates. One old lady says to the other, "Look at her, she's had her face lifted so often, when she raises her eyebrows her bedsocks shoot up her legs."

An old man is trying to get his friend to come out for a walk. "What happened to your get up and go?" he asks. "It got up and went without me," says his friend.

At the seaside there are two old men on their annual holidays standing in the sea with their trousers rolled up, smoking their pipes and watching the boats go by. One of them glances down at the other one's feet and says, "Blimey, mate, look at the state of your feet, they're absolutely filthy!" The other looks down and agrees, "Yeah, I know," he says. "We didn't manage to get here last year."

Albert and Henry are taking a stroll along the seafront one day when a seagull drops muck right on top of Albert's bald head. Henry says in great concern, "Wait right there. I'll be back in a moment." Henry hurries to the nearest public convenience and returns a few minutes later with a length of toilet paper. "It's a bit too late for that," says Albert. "That seagull will be miles away by now."

Two old ladies are in the park enjoying some music. "I think it's a minuet from Mignon," said one. "I thought it was a waltz from Faust," said the other. So one heads to a nearby notice board. "We were both wrong," she said. "It's a Refrain from Spitting."

Two old golfing partners are at the airport, booking a flight for a week's golfing holiday in sunny Spain. One of them, thinking about all the various things that could possibly go wrong, says, "Do you think we should take out any insurance?"

"No," replies the other one. "It's just a complete con, honestly. I never bother any more. I used to take it out, but it never seemed to make the slightest bit of difference."

A plane has a rough flight over the ocean. Suddenly the Captain's voice comes over the intercom: "Ladies and gentlemen, please fasten your seat belts and assume crash positions. We have lost our engines, but there's nothing to worry about, as we will be trying to put this baby down as smoothly and gently as possible for you on the water." "Oh stewardess! Are there any sharks in the ocean below?" asks a little old lady, terrified. The stewardess comes over to her with a kindly smile. "Yes, I'm afraid there are some sharks in this part of the ocean. But not to worry, we have a special gel in the bottle next to your chair designed especially for emergencies like this. Just rub the gel onto your arms and legs." "And if I do this, the sharks won't eat me any more?" asks the lady. "Oh, they'll still eat you all right," answers the stewardess. "But they won't enjoy it anywhere near as much."

Two old women, Millie and Dolly, are out driving through the town in a large car. Both can barely see over the dashboard. As they cruise along they come to a junction, and sail straight through a red light. Millie, in the passenger seat, thinks to herself, "I must be losing my mind, but I really could swear that we just went through a red light." After a few minutes they come to another intersection and go through another red light. Millie is almost sure that the light was red, but is again concerned that her memory might be playing tricks on her. At the next intersection they go through another red light, and a large 4x4 has to swerve suddenly to avoid crashing into them. The driver looks furious. Millie finally turns to Dolly and says "Dolly! Did you know we just ran through three red lights in a row! You could have killed us!" Dolly looks around startled and says, "Oh! Am I driving?"

Being 60 years old is like driving on the motorway at 50 miles an hour. Everybody seems to just pass you by.

A police officer is driving along one day when he sees an old lady in her car, driving along merrily while knitting furiously at the same time. The police man attempts unsuccessfully to get her attention, but to no avail, she doesn't notice. Finally he drives right alongside her, winds down his window and calls over, "Pull over, madam!" At which points the old lady turns to him and says, "It's socks actually, officer."

An elderly couple are driving when a police car pulls them over. "Do you realize you were speeding back there?" says the policeman. The woman being slightly deaf, turns to her husband and asks, "What did he say?" The old man shouts back, "He says you were speeding." The policeman says, "May I see your licence?" The old woman turns to her husband and asks, "What did he say." The old man shouts, "He wants to see your licence."

The woman ferrets around in her bag for a little while, and then hands over her licence. The officer says, "I see you're from Farnborough. I spent a bit of time there once. Do you know what? I had the worst sex I've ever had in my life with a woman in Farnborough. Oh she was a dreadful, unresponsive old bag!" The woman turns to her husband and asks, "What did he say?" The old man yells back, "He thinks he knows you!"

Police stop a car doing 20 on the motorway, and discover two little old ladies, one driving and one sitting in the passenger seat looking shaken and white as a sheet. "Now, madam," says one of the policemen to the driver, "why were you going so slowly?" "I always go at the speed that it says on the sign," explained the old woman. "And what sign was that madam?" asks the second policeman, fighting hard to keep a little smirk from his face. "It said M20," explained the little old lady. "So I did 20 miles an hour, the same way I did 31 miles an hour on the A31, then 40 miles an hour on the A40, and..." "I see the problem now, madam. What's wrong with your friend?" the policeman asks referring to the passenger who is still staring blankly into space. "Oh, you won't get any sense out of her," says the driver, "she's been like that ever since we came off the A159."

An ancient Ford pulls into a petrol station. "Could I have two litres of petrol?" asks the old driver. "Why don't you fill her up, now that you're here?" asks the attendant. "Well," says the old man, "she might not run that far."

A reporter visits a very old man on his birthday. "Have you lived in this town your whole life?" asks the reporter. "Obviously not," says the old man. "I haven't died yet, have I?"

An elderly couple go to a trendy restaurant to give themselves a treat, but they are turned away because it's full. They return the next night, but again it's full and they go home disappointed. The next night the same thing happens again. "Look," says the maitre d', "to save yourselves the time coming out here every night, why don't you just make a booking?" The old couple agree this would make sense, but are again disappointed to discover that the restaurant is booked solid for the next three weeks. "Tell you what," says the maitre d', "try phoning tomorrow. There might be a cancellation." The old man rings the next day and discovers that there haven't been any cancellations, and now the restaurant is booked solid for the next five weeks! The old man complains bitterly. "You know," he says, "your restaurant would do a lot more business if you weren't so bloody full all the time!"

Keith tells Harry, "We've recently had a terrible tragedy in our family. My grandmother died on her 99th birthday." "Oh no," says Harry. "That's really sad." "Yeah, I know," says Keith. "The worst thing is, we were only halfway through giving her the bumps at the time."

A man asks his wife what she'd like for her 40th birthday. She says she'd like to be six again. Next day the man buys his wife a party hat and a big sticky cake and hires a clown to show her some magic tricks and sings songs. The wife is unimpressed. "But you said you wanted to be six again," says the husband." "You idiot," she fumes. "I meant my dress size."

A wealthy old dowager goes to the National Gallery one day and tries to impress one of the attendants. "Oh, look!" she says. "Surely this a Goya?" "Er, no, madam, it's a Gainsborough actually," corrects the attendant. "Oh," says the woman glancing around hastily. "But that horrible, ugly, scary looking one; I know that for certain. It's The Scream by Edvard Munch." "No, madam," says the attendant. "That is in fact a mirror."

Two old ladies are visiting an art gallery one day and walk through the sculpture section. A few minutes later they emerge looking rather shocked and shaken. "Blimey!" says the first one. "Did you see that statue of that feller with the big doodah hanging out?" "Yes I did see that," says her friend. "Enormous wasn't it?" "I know," says the first one, "and it was so cold in there as well."

Old Tom tells Old Bert, "I was young once you know." "Cor!" says Bert. "You must have a good memory."

Two old men are talking over some sad memories. "You know it's 40 years today I lost my wife and children," says one. "Is it really?" says the other. "That's terrible." "Yes it is," says the first. "I'll never forget that poker game."

Four ladies are sitting playing bridge. The first lady says, "Girls, I've known you all many years and there's something I've got to get off my chest. I'm a kleptomaniac. I can't help it, I just have to steal things. I don't even really want them. I throw most of them away. But don't worry, I've never stolen from any of you, and I never will." The second lady pipes up, "Well, since we're confessing all, I might as well tell you that I'm a nymphomaniac. And you know what? I've had some really great times. But don't worry, I've never tried to seduce your husbands and I never would." "Well," says the third lady. "I've something to confess too. I'm actually a lesbian. But there's really no need to worry girls, you're just not my type." The fourth lady stands up. "Well, I have to confess too," she says. "I'm totally addicted to gossiping. Now, if you'll excuse me, I've got some phone calls to make."

An old man walks into a church to make his confession. "Forgive me father, for I have sinned," says the old man. "I am 80 years old and I was walking home from the pensioners' dinner club the other day when a couple of 20-year-old girls stopped their car and said they needed directions. We got into a discussion and they offered to drive me home. On the way one asked me the last time I'd had sex, so of course I told her, and you know what? It was before either of them were born! Then before I knew it we were all in my bed performing the most shocking erotic acts I've ever known." The priest sits tutting through all this. Finally he asks, "OK, so how long is it since your last confession?" "Never," says the old man. "I'm Jewish." "What do you mean?" says the priest. "If you're Jewish why are you telling me all this?" "I'm not just telling you," says the old man, "I'm telling everyone."

A new young priest is nervous about hearing confessions so he asks his older more experienced colleague to sit in with him on his sessions. The new priest hears a few confessions but then the old priest asks him to step out of the confessional for a moment. "OK," says the old priest, "when you hear confessions, rather than just slouching comfortably, try crossing your arms over your chest, and rubbing your chin with one hand. It'll make it look like you're deep in thought." The new priest tries this. Then the old priest suggests, "Also try saying things like, 'I see, yes, go on,' and 'I understand', or 'How did you feel about that?'" The new priest takes these suggestions on board as well. "And finally," says the old priest, "when you're hearing people confess their private, most intimate sins, try not to keep slapping your knee and saying, "Wow! Cool, man! So what happened next?"

An elderly man bought a large farm in Florida and fixed it up with walkways, orchards, tennis courts and a pond at the furthest edge of the property. One evening he decided to go down to the pond and took a bucket with him to bring back some fruit. As he got nearer, he heard voices shouting and laughing with glee. As he came closer he saw a bunch of young women skinny dipping in his pond. He made the women aware of his presence with a loud cough, and they all immediately dived for the deep end. One of the women shouted to him, "Hey, you old pervert! We're not coming out of here until you leave!" "That's OK," said the old man, "I didn't come down here to watch you ladies swim naked – or make you get out of the pond naked either, for that matter." Then he held up his bucket and said, "Fact is, I'm just down here to feed my alligator!"

A vicar is walking through his parish one day and stops to admire an area that an elderly parishioner has turned from a piece of wasteland into a beautiful garden. "Ah," says the vicar, "It's so inspiring what man can achieve with the help of the Almighty," "Yes," replies the old man. "Indeed it is, vicar. But you should have seen the mess it was in when He had it all to Himself."

Two elderly women gardeners enter their carrots in the village vegetable show. One is declared the winner and starts crowing about her success. "Well, I'm not surprised I won, to be honest," she says. "Your carrots were a bit on the small side, quite frankly." "That's true," says the other woman. "They could have been quite a lot bigger. Mind you, my dear, I did grow them to fit my mouth, not yours."

An elderly gentleman walks into a West End furriers with a young lady on his arms and says he wants to buy her a mink coat costing £15,000. "Will a cheque be OK?" asks the man. "Certainly, sir," says the sales assistant. "But we'll have to wait a few days for it to clear before we're able to release the goods to you. I'm sure you understand. Can you come back on Monday to take delivery?" "Certainly," replies the old man, and he and his girlfriend walk out arm in arm. Next Monday the man returns to the shop as promised. The sales assistant is furious, "You've got a nerve coming back here. It turns out there's hardly a penny in your bank account. Your cheque was completely worthless." "Yes, I know. Sorry about that," replies the man. "I just came in to apologize... and to thank you for your help in setting up what has to be the greatest weekend of my life."

A rambler sees an old farmer staring intently at a small length of rope. "Good afternoon," says the rambler. "Tell me, what's that piece of rope for?" "I can use it to tell the weather," says the old farmer. "Really?" says the rambler, impressed. "How does it work?" "Well," says the farmer, "when the rope shifts slightly from side to side, that means it's windy. And when it feels wet, that means it's raining."

A man and his wife are looking out of the back window at lavish and well-trimmed vegetable patch in the back garden. The wife turns to the husband and says, "You know, Bert, sooner or later you're going to have to make a proper scarecrow for this place." "Why?" asks her husband. "Because," she says, "I'm absolutely certain that your poor mother's arms must be getting awfully tired by now."

Little Billy is very happy to see his grandmother come to visit again. He runs up, gives her a hug and tells her, "I'm so happy to see you, Grandma. Now Daddy will have to do that trick he's been promising to do." "What trick is that, dear?" asks his grandmother. "Well," says little Billy, "Daddy told us he would climb up the flipping wall if you came to visit us again."

A grandmother buys a toy water cannon for her three-year-old grandson. When the little boy opens his present his dad says to the grandmother, "I'm really surprised you'd buy him something like that. Don't you remember how I used to drive you mad firing my water cannon at you when I was little? You used to absolutely hate the damn thing." "Yes," says the grandmother with a wicked smile. "I remember very well indeed."

An 80-year-old man is going through customs at the airport when he is pulled over for a random search. "Excuse me, sir," says the official, "do you mind telling me how old you are?" "I'm 40," says the man. "Sir," says the official, "according to your passport, you're 80 years old." "Yes," says the old man, "but I was married for 40 years of that and you don't call that living do you?"

Have you ever thought, in 40 years' time when they're going over all the things they had to do without when they were young, what exactly are the children of today going to moan about?

Two women are discussing a mutual friend. "She's not pushing 40," says one. "No," says the other, "She's most definitely not. She's clinging on to the damned thing for dear life."

A doctor begins his examination of an old man by asking him what brought him to the hospital. "Er," says the old man. "That's a good question. I think it might have been an ambulance, actually."

An old lady goes to the doctor's for a check-up. The doctor asks her how she's doing, and receives a litany of complaints about her aches and pains. "Now come on, Mrs Siegel," says the doctor. "You have to expect things to start deteriorating at your age. After all, who wants to live to be 100?" The old lady gives him a cold look and replies, "I would have thought anyone who's 99."

Did you hear about the old man whose health was so bad his doctor advised him not to start watching any new series?

A middle-aged man is due to have an operation and is very worried about it, so just before he tells the surgeon that he's rather nervous and concerned. "You see, doctor," he says, "I've heard that only one in ten people survives this particular operation. Is that true?" "Unfortunately yes," admits the surgeon. "That is correct. But looking on the bright side you've got nothing to worry about, because my last nine patients all died!"

A very forgetful old man goes to a singles bar and tries to pick up women by going up to them and saying, "Hello. Do I come here often?"

A very old man, almost bent double, hobbles up to an ice-cream seller and asks for a vanilla cone. "Crushed nuts, mate?" asks the seller. "No," says the old man. "It's rheumatism, if you must know."

For a long time old Tom's family thought he had become hunchbacked due to his advancing years. Eventually though they found out that it was just because he didn't know his braces were adjustable.

An old man tells a friend, "I just bought myself a new hearing aid. It cost me £4,000, but it's state of the art." "Great," says his friend. "What kind is it?" "12.30."

An old man goes to a wizard to ask him if he can remove a horrible curse that has been ruining his life for the last 40 years. The wizard think about it and says, "If you can tell me the exact words that were used to put the curse on you, I should be able to free you." The old man says, without hesitation, "I now pronounce you man and wife."

Two old women are watching their husbands. "I can't believe your husband is still chasing after women," says one. "Doesn't worry me," says the other. "Even if he somehow did manage to catch one of them, he wouldn't be able to remember what he wanted her for."

If you're a woman and you get called in for a mammogram, look on the bright side. At least this is one kind of film they still want you to appear topless in.

A middle-aged woman goes to the doctor for a check-up and comes back delighted. "What are you so happy about?" asks her husband grumpily. "The doctor said I have the body of a 25-year-old," she replies. "OK," says her husband, "but what did he say about your 45-year-old arse?" "Ah yeah, I'm glad you asked me that actually. I'm afraid he didn't mention you at all," says the wife sweetly.

An old man is buying organic vegetables. He asks one stallholder, "These vegetables are for my wife. Have they been sprayed with poisonous chemicals?" "No," says the market trader. "You'll have to do that yourself."

Do you know, for as long as I can remember I've had amnesia.